GUIDED FILL

MY MOM
ROCKS

101 REASONS WHY I LOVE YOU, MOM

YOU WILL ROCK BOOKS

DEDICATION

To my Mom,

I am so blessed to have you as my mom in this lifetime.

You are the strongest person I know, the most resilient, and the goofiest.

I hope you enjoy each page of this book.

You are the best mom ever.

I love you to the moon and back!

DEAR,

_____

This journal is for you.

Here are 101 reasons why I love you, Mom.

LOVE,

_____

HOW TO USE THIS BOOK

Hi, there!

This is the book speaking to you.

All of my prompts are fill-in-the-blank, so you can start on any page!

The only rule is to be creative and have fun.

Now go show your mom how much you love her!

BONUS: MY GIFT TO YOU

One last thing before we get started.

To keep this short and sweet, I wanted to give you something.

You've already done more than most by buying your mom this book and showing her your gratitude.

So, the least I could do is give you this free guide on **14 crazy simple DIY gifts for mom.**

BONUS:
MY GIFT TO YOU

Scan the QR code
below to access it.

All right, enough chit-chat.

Let's dive in for real this time!

MEMORIES

The memorable ones.

"AND YET MEMORIES ARE THE MOST PRECIOUS THINGS WE'LL EVER HAVE."

-UNKNOWN

My Mom Rocks **Photo Time!**

MEMORIES

My Mom Rocks   **Memories**

1. MY FAVORITE MEMORY WITH YOU HAS TO BE

_____

_____

_____

2. THREE QUALITIES I ADMIRE IN YOU ARE

1 _____

2 _____

3 _____

My Mom Rocks   **Memories**

3. SOMETHING I LEARNED FROM YOU THAT I USE EVERY DAY IS

_____

_____

_____

4. A SONG THAT REMINDS ME SO MUCH OF YOU IS

_____ BECAUSE _____

_____

_____

_____

My Mom Rocks **Memories**

5. ONE OF THE FUNNIEST MOMENTS WE'VE SHARED IS WHEN

_____

_____

_____

6. THREE THINGS YOU'VE TAUGHT ME THAT I'M MOST GRATEFUL FOR ARE

1. _____

2. _____

3. _____

My Mom Rocks   **Memories**

7. THE SMELL THAT REMINDS ME OF YOU WHENEVER I PASS IT IS _____ BECAUSE

_____

_____

8. THE HAPPIEST I'VE EVER SEEN YOU WAS WHEN

_____

_____

_____

_____

My Mom Rocks **Memories**

9. WHEN I THINK OF YOU, THE FIRST THING THAT COMES TO MIND IS

_____

_____

_____

10. A MOVIE OR SHOW THAT REMINDS ME OF YOU IS

_____ **BECAUSE** _____

_____

_____

_____

My Mom Rocks   **Memories**

11. IF I COULD FREEZE ONE MOMENT IN TIME WITH YOU, IT WOULD BE

_____

_____

_____

12. A TIME YOU MADE ME LAUGH SO HARD WAS

_____ **BECAUSE** _____

_____

_____

_____

My Mom Rocks   **Memories**

13. A TIME WHEN YOU MADE ME FEEL INVINCIBLE WAS

_____

_____

_____

14. IF I COULD BE MORE LIKE YOU IN A SILLY WAY, IT WOULD BE

_____

_____

_____

15. A PHRASE YOU SAY THAT I'LL NEVER FORGET IS

_____

_____

_____

16. GROWING UP, MY FAVORITE FAMILY GET-TOGETHER WAS

_____

_____

_____

_____

My Mom Rocks   **Memories**

17. A SPECIAL TRADITION WE HAVE THAT I LOVE IS

_____

_____

_____

18. IF I COULD DESCRIBE YOU IN ONE WORD, IT WOULD BE _____ BECAUSE

_____

_____

_____

_____

My Mom Rocks Memories

19. THE THING I APPRECIATE MOST ABOUT YOU IS

_____

_____

_____

20. A MOMENT I'VE NEVER STOPPED LAUGHING ABOUT IS WHEN YOU

_____

_____

_____

_____

My Mom Rocks   **Memories**

21. ONE THING YOU ALWAYS SAY THAT MAKES ME SMILE IS

_____

_____

_____

22. A TIME WHEN YOU MADE ME FEEL INCREDIBLY LOVED WAS

_____

_____

_____

My Mom Rocks   **Memories**

23. YOUR BEST ADVICE ABOUT LIFE WAS

_____

_____

_____

24. A MEMORY I'LL NEVER FORGET GROWING UP HAS TO BE

_____

_____

_____

_____

HUMOR

The funny ones.

WHAT DO YOU CALL A PANDA THAT TELLS JOKES?

"A PUN-DA!"

My Mom Rocks   **Photo Time!**

HUMOR

My Mom Rocks Humor

25. THE SILLIEST THING YOU'VE EVER DONE WAS

_____

_____

_____

26. IF I COULD DESCRIBE YOUR LAUGH, I'D SAY IT'S KINDA LIKE

_____

_____

_____

_____

My Mom Rocks   Humor

27. IF MOM JOKES WERE A COMPETITION, YOUR BEST ONE WOULD BE

_____

_____

_____

28. IF I COULD RENAME YOU BASED ON YOUR PERSONALITY, YOUR NEW NAME WOULD BE

_____

_____

_____

_____

My Mom Rocks   **Humor**

29. A LAUGHING MOMENT I'LL NEVER FORGET WITH YOU WAS WHEN

_____

_____

_____

30. YOU'VE MASTERED THE SUBTLE ART OF

_____

_____

_____

_____

My Mom Rocks **Humor**

31. IF_____ WERE A CURRENCY, YOU'D BE A BILLIONAIRE FOR THE WAY YOU HANDLE

_____

_____

_____

32. THE MOST RIDICULOUS ADVICE YOU'VE EVER GIVEN ME (THAT ACTUALLY WORKED) WAS

_____

_____

_____

My Mom Rocks   **Humor**

33. YOUR CRAZIEST HALLOWEEN COSTUME THAT EMBARRASSED ME THE MOST WAS

_____

_____

_____

34. THE TIME YOU _____

_____

INSTEAD OF _____

_____

_____ **WAS SO MOM OF YOU.**

My Mom Rocks   **Humor**

35. IF THERE WERE AN OLYMPIC EVENT FOR

_____

_____

_____

YOU'D TAKE HOME THE GOLD MEDAL!

36. A TIME YOU EMBARRASSED ME (IN THE BEST WAY) WAS

_____

_____

_____

_____

My Mom Rocks   **Humor**

37. THE BEST "MOM JOKE" YOU'VE EVER TOLD ME WAS

_____

_____

_____

38. THE MOST SILLY THING ABOUT YOU THAT I ABSOLUTELY LOVE IS

_____

_____

_____

_____

My Mom Rocks Humor

39. IF THERE WERE AN AWARD FOR

_____

_____

_____

YOU'D WIN IT HANDS DOWN.

40. YOUR MOST "CREATIVE" PARENTING RULE WAS

_____

_____

_____

AND IT STILL DOESN'T MAKE SENSE!

My Mom Rocks   **Humor**

41. IF THERE WERE A "WORLD'S _____ _____ MOM" TROPHY, YOU'D WIN IT BECAUSE

_____

_____

42. NOW THAT I'M OLDER, IT'S TIME I TELL YOU ABOUT

_____

_____

_____

_____

My Mom Rocks   **Humor**

43. I CAN'T GET OVER THAT ONE TIME YOU

_____

_____

_____

44. IF I COULD SWAP BODIES WITH YOU FOR ONE DAY I WOULD DO

_____

_____

_____

My Mom Rocks   **Humor**

45. THE MOST I'VE SEEN YOU SWEAT WAS WHEN YOU

_____

_____

_____

46. THE MOST "DRAMA QUEEN" THING THAT YOU'VE EVER SAID TO ME WAS

_____

_____

_____

_____

My Mom Rocks   **Humor**

47. IF I HAD TO EXPLAIN YOUR PERSONALITY USING ONLY SOUND EFFECTS, IT WOULD SOUND LIKE

_____

_____

_____

48. REMEMBER IN PUBLIC, THAT ONE TIME WHEN YOU

_____

_____

_____

My Mom Rocks Humor

49. AS I GREW OLDER, THE MOST SURPRISING THING I LEARNED ABOUT YOU IS

_____

_____

_____

50. YOU'VE TAUGHT ME HOW TO FIND LAUGHTER IN

_____

_____

_____

GRATITUDE

The grateful ones.

"THE MORE GRATEFUL I AM, THE MORE BEAUTY I SEE."

–MARY DAVIS

My Mom Rocks   Photo Time!

GRATITUDE

My Mom Rocks   **Gratitude**

51. YOU MADE ME FEEL PROUD WHEN YOU

_____

_____

_____

52. ONE SENTENCE THAT DESCRIBES OUR RELATIONSHIP IS

_____

_____

_____

_____

My Mom Rocks   **Gratitude**

53. A WAY YOU'VE MADE MY LIFE BETTER IS

_____

_____

_____

54. IF I COULD THANK YOU FOR JUST ONE THING, IT WOULD BE

_____

_____

_____

_____

My Mom Rocks   Gratitude

55. I ADMIRE YOUR _____

_____

_____

MORE THAN ANYTHING.

56. ONE OF YOUR HABITS I HOPE TO ADOPT IS

_____

_____

_____

_____

My Mom Rocks   **Gratitude**

57. THE BEST PART OF SPENDING TIME WITH YOU IS

_____

_____

_____

58. THREE OF YOUR SUPERPOWERS HAVE TO BE

1 _____

2 _____

3 _____

My Mom Rocks   **Gratitude**

59. IF I COULD BORROW ONE OF YOUR SKILLS FOR A DAY, IT WOULD BE YOUR ABILITY TO

_____

_____

_____

60. A PIECE OF ADVICE YOU GAVE ME THAT I'LL DEFINITELY PASS DOWN IS

_____

_____

_____

My Mom Rocks   **Gratitude**

61. YOU'VE INSPIRED ME TO

_____

_____

_____

62. THE BEST STORY YOU'VE EVER TOLD WAS

_____

_____

_____

_____

My Mom Rocks Gratitude

63. SOMETHING YOU'VE DONE THAT AMAZED ME WAS

_____

_____

_____

64. I KNOW I CAN ALWAYS COUNT ON YOU FOR

_____

_____

_____

_____

My Mom Rocks   **Gratitude**

65. THE KINDEST THING YOU'VE EVER DONE FOR ME IS

_____

_____

_____

66. I'M SO GRATEFUL YOU TAUGHT ME HOW TO

_____

_____

_____

_____

My Mom Rocks   Gratitude

67. I ALWAYS THINK OF YOU WHEN I SEE

_____

_____

_____

68. ONE THING YOU DO BETTER THAN ANYONE ELSE HAS TO BE

_____

_____

_____

_____

My Mom Rocks   **Gratitude**

69. A HOBBY OR SKILL I'VE PICKED UP BECAUSE OF YOU IS

_____

_____

_____

70. YOU MAKE ME FEEL SAFE WHEN

_____

_____

_____

_____

My Mom Rocks Gratitude

71. YOU'RE THE ONLY PERSON WHO CAN MAKE ME SMILE EVEN WHEN

_____

_____

_____

72. YOUR KINDNESS DURING _____

_____

_____

_____

SHOWED ME WHAT IT TRULY MEANS TO CARE FOR SOMEONE.

My Mom Rocks   Gratitude

73. THE BEST ADVICE YOU'VE GIVEN ME ABOUT HAPPINESS IS

_____

_____

_____

_____

74. IF I COULD BOTTLE YOUR WISDOM, THE LABEL WOULD SAY

_____

_____

AND THE INSTRUCTIONS WOULD READ, "USE FOR…

_____

_____

My Mom Rocks   Gratitude

75. A TIME WHEN YOUR WORDS COMPLETELY CHANGED MY DAY WAS WHEN

_____

_____

_____

76. YOUR HUGS REMIND ME OF

_____

_____

_____

LOVE

The lovey ones.

"ALL THAT I AM I OWE TO YOU. I LOVE YOU, MOM."

-UNKOWN

My Mom Rocks   **Photo Time!**

LOVE

My Mom Rocks   Love

77. YOU'VE TAUGHT ME TO ALWAYS REMEMBER

_____

_____

_____

78. A TIME YOU FORGAVE ME WHEN I DIDN'T DESERVE IT WAS

_____

_____

_____

_____

My Mom Rocks   **Love**

79. YOUR BIGGEST STRENGTH, IN MY OPINION, IS

_____

_____

_____

80. ONE OF MY FAVORITE THINGS I LOVE ABOUT YOU IS

_____

_____

_____

_____

My Mom Rocks   **Love**

81. I'VE NEVER TOLD YOU THIS BEFORE, BUT I LOVE

_____

_____

_____

82. IF I COULD TELL THE WORLD ONE THING ABOUT YOU, IT WOULD BE

_____

_____

_____

My Mom Rocks   Love

83. A TRADITION YOU STARTED THAT I'LL ALWAYS CARRY FORWARD IS

_____

_____

_____

84. THE WAY YOU'VE SUPPORTED ME DURING

_____

_____

_____

MADE ME REALIZE HOW MUCH YOU BELIEVE IN ME.

My Mom Rocks   **Love**

85. YOU'VE MADE ME APPRECIATE THE BEAUTY OF

_____

_____

_____

86. A QUIET MOMENT WE SHARED THAT I'LL NEVER FORGET IS

_____

_____

_____

My Mom Rocks   Love

87. ONE WAY YOU'VE SHOWN YOUR LOVE IS BY

_____

_____

_____

88. A TIME YOU GAVE ME CONFIDENCE WAS WHEN

_____

_____

_____

_____

My Mom Rocks   **Love**

89. IF I COULD TIME-TRAVEL WITH YOU TO SOMEWHERE THAT WE BOTH LOVE, IT WOULD BE TO

_____

_____

_____

90. YOU MAKE LIFE BEAUTIFUL BY

_____

_____

_____

_____

My Mom Rocks Love

91. IF I COULD CHOOSE ONE LESSON FROM YOU TO TEACH THE WORLD, IT WOULD BE

_____

_____

_____

92. SOMETHING SMALL YOU'VE DONE THAT MEANS THE WORLD TO ME IS

_____

_____

_____

_____

My Mom Rocks   **Love**

93. IF I COULD GIVE YOU A STANDING OVATION FOR ONE THING, IT WOULD BE FOR

_____

_____

_____

94. IF I COULD DESCRIBE YOUR IMPACT ON MY LIFE IN ONE SENTENCE, IT WOULD BE:

_____

_____

_____

My Mom Rocks   Love

95. IF I COULD CREATE A NATIONAL HOLIDAY FOR YOU, IT WOULD BE CALLED

_____

AND WE'D CELEBRATE IT BY

_____

_____

96. THE SWEETEST ACT OF LOVE YOU'VE EVER SHOW ME WAS WHEN

_____

_____

_____

My Mom Rocks   **Love**

97. YOU'VE SHOWN ME HOW TO CHERISH

_____

_____

_____

98. IF I COULD THANK YOU A MILLION TIMES FOR ONE THING, IT WOULD BE

_____

_____

_____

My Mom Rocks   Love

99. IF I COULD WRITE A BOOK ABOUT YOU, THE TITLE WOULD BE

_____

_____

_____

100. IF I COULD DESCRIBE THE FEELING OF YOUR LOVE, IT WOULD FEEL LIKE

_____

_____

_____

SPECIAL

The special one.

MY MOM ROCKS! HERE ARE 101 REASONS WHY I LOVE YOU, MOM

-LEXI KAZ

My Mom Rocks   **Photo Time!**

SPECIAL

My Mom Rocks   **Special**

101. I LOVE YOU MOM BECAUSE

_____

_____

_____

_____

_____

A FINAL THANK YOU

_____

_____

_____

_____

LOVE,

_____

#1 MOM OF THE YEAR AWARD

We hope you enjoyed completing this book!

You've given your mom something she'll love forever.

So I have **one** last question for you.

Do you feel she's the **#1 Mom of the Year?**

Hopefully, you said yes!

#1 MOM OF THE YEAR AWARD

If you did say yes, please do the following!

1. Post a video of your mom's reaction to giving her this book

2. Tag us on **TikTok @Youwillrockbooks**

3. Mention why you believe she deserves to win the **#1 Mom of the Year Award.**

The winner will receive a cash prize from **You Will Rock Books** to further our mission of supporting Mothers everywhere.

#1 MOM OF THE YEAR AWARD

The best video submission will win the **#1 Mom of the Year Award.**

Now go give her this book!

For more information on the **#1 Mom of the Year Award**, go to www.Youwillrock.com

Or email us any questions at info@youwillrock.com

PASS IT ON!

If you enjoyed our book, please leave us an honest review from wherever you purchased it.

This way, another Mom can get the gratitude she deserves!

THE END.